What Living Things Do

By Jennifer Nwokeji and Kene Nwokeji

Illustrated by Anak Bulu

Dedicated to all my teachers from preschool to third grade, especially
Ms. Barrett and Ms. Wasyliszyn, for teaching me lots of Science and Literacy.

Special thanks to Dad and Mom for always being my first teachers.
I love you. I love you too, Kaine, my baby brother.

Kene Nwokeji

For bulk orders and special discounts contact:
www.instagram.com/jennwokeji
abchomeworkplace@gmail.com

ISBN: 978-1-7378232-5-4 (paperback)
Library of Congress Control Number: 2022910832
First Edition: July 2022

This book belongs to

Dubem had so many unanswered questions. "Mom, why do trees lose their leaves?"
"Trees are living things. Trees lose their leaves because they are SENSITIVE to the changes in their environment. That's what living things do," Mom said.

"Just like trees and animals, your body is sensitive to its environment, too. I can see that you are cold. Let's go home," Dad added.

"Why do I have to eat?" Dubem asked.
"You eat because you are a living thing, and that's what living things do," Mom said. "Your body needs NUTRITION for all the activities of the day. Food helps you grow, gives you energy, and helps your body fight diseases."

"Do plants eat, too?"
"Yes they do, from sunlight, carbon dioxide in the air, and water in the soil," Mom said. "Now, eat up!"

"Why do I have to poop?" Dubem asked.
"You poop because you are a living thing, and that's what living things do,"
Mom said. "Urinating, defecating, sweating, and exhaling carbon dioxide are
ways for your body to **EXCRETE** waste and stay healthy."

"Do plants poop, too?"
"Plants don't poop like humans and animals," Mom laughed, "But during the
day, plants exhale oxygen for us humans and animals to breathe. You'll
have to ask Ms. Johnson or Google about plants defecating."

"You GROW because you are a living thing, and that's what living things do," Dad said. "Inside you are cells that make you grow, change, and get older. And that's why you should wear these pajamas instead."

"Do plants grow, too?"

"Yes, plants grow," Dad said. "Remember that our garden flowers started as seeds. Most trees start as seeds, too."

"Why do I feel sleepy?" Dubem asked.
"You feel sleepy because your body is responding to how tired it is.
When you sleep, your body uses the food you eat to grow bigger
and stronger," Dad said.

snore!
snore!
snore!
snore!
?

"Do plants sleep, too?"
"Not exactly, but they are less active when the sun sets.
Just like you, the energy plants get during the day, is used to
grow taller and bigger at night," Dad yawned. "Now go to sleep.
I am tired, too."

"Why do I breathe in air?" Dubem asked. "You breathe in air or RESPIRE because you are a living thing, and that's what living things do," Mom said.

"Air keeps you alive. You breathe in oxygen and breathe out carbon dioxide. Animals and plants breathe, too. Plants breathe by photosynthesis during the day, and by cellular respiration at night.

"Did you notice people and animals moving around? People and animals MOVE because they are living things, and that's what living things do. People and animals move to get what they need to survive.

Plants move too! They move very slowly toward the sun. Their roots spread very slowly underground to find water and nutrients in the soil."

"Why did you and Dad have Nedu and I?" Dubem asked.
"We had you and Nedu because we love you two," Mom said. "Living things are able to REPRODUCE young ones of their own kind. That's what living things do. You'll see, Ms. Johnson's baby will look just like Ms. Johnson."

"I love you too, Mom. And don't worry, I know that plants reproduce, too. Dad already told me."

"Good morning, Dubem. We have a new unit to discuss today – Living Things and Non-living Things," Ms. Johnson said.

"Good morning, Ms. Johnson, I know about living things; my parents taught me. But I'm yet to learn about non-living things. Will you teach me, please?" Dubem asked.

"I sure will! Just remember that non-living things cannot MRS. GREN."

Hello friend,

I present to you, MRS. GREN, the characteristics of living things!

Plants, animals, and humans are living things. They have the characteristics that go by the acronym, MRS. GREN. Micro organisms like bacteria, fungi, and viruses are living things, too. Non-living things are inanimate objects like stones, tables, cloth, or books; they do not have the characteristics of living things. Take a look around you. What is living and non-living? Use the checklist to help you with your answer.

From,
Dubem

Living or Non-Living Checklist

	M	R	S	G	R	E	N	Living / Non-Living
Teddy	✗	✗	✗	✗	✗	✗	✗	Non-Living
Grass	✓	✓	✓	✓	✓	✓	✓	Living

Glossary

acronym: a word formed by using the first letters of a group of things.	Google: a search website found on the internet.
carbon dioxide: air that is breathed out of humans and animals.	kind: the same group of things with similar features.
cells: the smallest units of life found inside living things.	nutrition: food meant for the body.
cellular respiration: the process when plants take in oxygen and let out carbon dioxide.	oxygen: the air living things breathe to stay alive.
characteristics: the features that describe something or a group of things.	photosynthesis: the process when plants use carbon dioxide, water, and sunlight to make their food.
defecating: when the body passes out a soft substance called feces or poop.	respire: to breathe air in and out of the body.
diseases: illnesses that causes harm to the body.	reproduce: to make or create something.
environment: one's surroundings at any time.	sensitive: being able to feel and respond to what happens inside the body and in the environment.
excrete: to pass waste products out of the body.	survive: to live and stay alive.
exhale: to remove air from the lungs through the nose or mouth.	urinating: when the body passes out a yellowish liquid called urine or pee.

Kene Nwokeji is the co-author of What Living Things Do. At the end of third grade, Kene marked the end of his early childhood education by living his dream of writing his first book. Kene enjoys doing science experiments, playing outdoors, and reading nonfiction books.

Jennifer Nwokeji is a wife, teacher, and mother to Kene and Kaine Nwokeji. She has authored children's books that focus on emotional intelligence and general knowledge. Jennifer enjoys spending time with her family, doing arts and craft, and working with children.

Other books by Jennifer Nwokeji

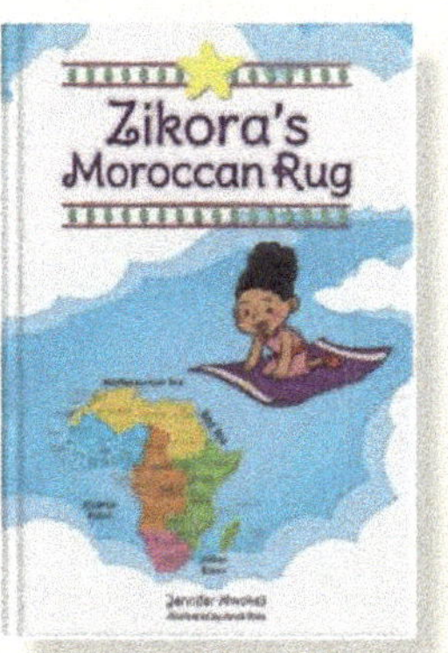